For The

Serious Collector

Record Journal Book

Activinotes

Activinotes

DAILY JOURNALS, PLANNERS, NOTEBOOKS AND OTHER BLANK BOOKS

What my collection looks like

Date: ____________

What my collection looks like

Date: __________

My latest collection

What my collection looks like

Date: ____________

What my collection looks like

Date: ______________

My latest collection

What my collection looks like

Date: ____________

What my collection looks like

Date: ______________

My latest collection

What my collection looks like

Date: ____________

What my collection looks like

Date: ______________

My latest collection

What my collection looks like

Date:

What my collection looks like

Date: ____________

My latest collection

What my collection looks like

Date: ____________

What my collection looks like

Date: ____________

My latest collection

What my collection looks like

Date: ______________

What my collection looks like

Date: ______

My latest collection

What my collection looks like

Date: ____________

What my collection looks like

Date: ______________

My latest collection

What my collection looks like

Date: ____________

What my collection looks like

Date: ____________

My latest collection

What my collection looks like

Date: ____________

What my collection looks like

Date: ____________

My latest collection

What my collection looks like

Date: ____________

What my collection looks like

Date: ______________

My latest collection

What my collection looks like

Date: ______________

What my collection looks like

Date: ______________

My latest collection

What my collection looks like

Date: ______________

What my collection looks like

Date: ____________

My latest collection

What my collection looks like

Date: ____________

What my collection looks like

Date: ___________

My latest collection

What my collection looks like

Date: ______________

What my collection looks like

Date: ______________

My latest collection

What my collection looks like

Date: ______________

What my collection looks like

Date: ______________

My latest collection

What my collection looks like

Date: ____________

What my collection looks like

Date: ______________

My latest collection

What my collection looks like

Date: ____________

What my collection looks like

Date: ______________

My latest collection

What my collection looks like

Date: ______________

What my collection looks like

Date: ____________

My latest collection

What my collection looks like

Date: ______________

What my collection looks like

Date: ______________

My latest collection

What my collection looks like

Date: ______________

What my collection looks like

Date: ______

My latest collection

What my collection looks like

Date: ______________

What my collection looks like

Date: ____________

My latest collection

What my collection looks like

Date: ____________

What my collection looks like

Date: ____________

My latest collection

What my collection looks like

Date: ______________

What my collection looks like

Date: ____________

My latest collection

What my collection looks like

Date: ______________

What my collection looks like

Date: ______________

My latest collection

What my collection looks like

Date: ______________

What my collection looks like

Date: ____________

My latest collection

What my collection looks like

Date: ____________

What my collection looks like

Date: ____________

My latest collection

What my collection looks like

Date: ______

What my collection looks like

Date: ______________

My latest collection

What my collection looks like

Date: ____________

What my collection looks like

Date: ____________

My latest collection

What my collection looks like

Date: ____________

What my collection looks like

Date: ____________

My latest collection

What my collection looks like

Date: ____________

What my collection looks like

Date: ______________

My latest collection

What my collection looks like

Date: ______________

Date:

Scripture for the day:

My meditative thoughts:

My latest collection

What my collection looks like

Date: ______________

What my collection looks like

Date: ____________

Well, that's what life is - this collection of extraordinarily ordinary moments. We just need to pay attention to them all. Wake up and pay attention to how beautiful it all is.

Alexander Payne

www.ingramcontent.com/pod-product-compliance
Lightning Source LLC
Chambersburg PA
CBHW080720290626
47170CB00017B/2868
* 9 7 8 1 6 8 3 2 1 0 5 5 9 *